HOW BEAUTIFUL THE BELOVED

HOW BEAUTIFUL
THE BELOVED

Gregory Orr

Copper Canyon Press

Copper Canyon Press is in residence at Fort Worden State Park
in Port Townsend, Washington, under the auspices of Centrum.
Centrum is a gathering place for artists and creative thinkers
from around the world, students of all ages and backgrounds,
and audiences seeking extraordinary cultural enrichment.

Some of these poems appeared in *The American Poetry Review,*
Columbia, Image, MARGIE, Poetry International, Smartish Pace,
Quarry West, and *The Virginia Quarterly Review.*

LIBRARY OF CONGRESS CATALOGING-IN-PUBLICATION DATA

Orr, Gregory.
How beautiful the beloved / Gregory Orr.
p. cm.
ISBN 978-1-55659-283-6 (alk. paper)
I. Title.
PS3565.R7H69 2009, 2019
811'.54–dc22
2008040970

COPPER CANYON PRESS
Post Office Box 271
Port Townsend, Washington 98368
www.coppercanyonpress.org

FOR TRISHA

CONTENTS

PART ONE

PART TWO

PART THREE

PART FOUR

HOW BEAUTIFUL THE BELOVED

PART ONE

✤ If to say it once
And once only, then still
To say: Yes.

And say it complete,
Say it as if the word
Filled the whole moment
With its absolute saying.

Later for "but,"
Later for "if."
                    Now
Only the single syllable
That is the beloved,
That is the world.

❧ The Book said we were mortal;
   It didn't say we had to be morbid.

   The Book said the beloved died,
   But also that she comes again,
   That he's reborn as words.

   The Book said: Everything perishes.
   The Book said: That's why we sing.

❋ How we embraced the beloved
So tightly that fate itself
Was changed into destiny.

Then everything was different.

Exactly as before, but also
Different.
            Death still there,
But different.
                Loss still
Omnipresent, but not the same.

Held in our arms, holding us
Even as she vanished,
Even as he turned into song.

❊ And when the beloved
Is a person
So much the better,
So much the worse.

You'll know no peace.
Misery will be your pillow
And you will not sleep.

So much the better:
Staying up all night
Talking to her,
Thinking about him.

So much the worse:
Where is she now?
Where, in this wide world,
Is he wandering?

❧ How beautiful
The beloved.

Whether garbed
In mortal tatters,
Or in her dress
Of everlastingness –

Moon broken
On the water,
Or moon
Still whole
In the night sky.

❧ Balanced on the edge
Of speech,
But the slope is so steep.

To speak is to leap.
Wanting to, but afraid.

Instead, merely
Gazing at the beloved
From that tall cliff.

❧ *Si je t'aime, prends garde à toi!*
Sings Carmen in Bizet's opera:
"If I love you, watch out!"
Good advice: she's dangerous.
Love is dangerous.

                    As is the world.
It isn't only loss – there's lots
Of weird malice loose on the planet.

Of course, her song is in the Book;
Not as a warning but an invitation.
"Welcome," it says, "but be alert."

✢ Where are you standing
That you can pluck
What you love
From the flood?

On the Book—more
Solid than any rock,
Rock being only
A slower flowing.

❧ Don't bother to ask
For the Book at the library:
It's always checked out.
You'd have to conclude
No one ever returns it.

Better to put together
Your own version:
The poems and songs
You love – the ones
That saved you when
You were young
And suffered.
        And also
Those that consoled you
When you were older.

❦ Not many of them, it's true,
But certain poems
In an uncertain world –
The ones we cling to:

They bring us back
Always to the beloved
Whom we thought we'd lost.

As surely as if the words
Led her by the hand,
Brought him before us.

Certain poems
In an uncertain world.

✤ A thousand years ago,
   A poet glimpsed
   The beloved
   And felt his eyes
   Fill with tears,
   Felt his mouth
   Become a smile.

   From what depths
   Inside you
   Do they rise
   As you read
   That poem aloud –
   Those tears
   In *your* eyes now,
   That same smile.

✣ Praxilla, almost-forgotten
 Greek poet – that poem
 She put in the Book.

 It concerns dead Achilles,
 And some considered it
 Undignified – the way
 She had him speak to us
 From that cheerless
 Afterworld the Greeks
 Imagined, even
 For their heroes – speak
 Of what he missed –
 Her poem a little list:

 Stars and moon and sun
 And the taste of ripe cucumbers.

❧ Snow on the mountain
This January morning,
Though the sky's blue.
Must have fallen
Last night.

More gray hairs
On my head
Every month.
My mustache
Almost completely
White now.

Too many funerals;
Not enough weddings.
Not enough birth
Announcements.

I hope the beloved
Isn't losing ground.

❧ Death of the body –
How many poems
In the Book
Urge us
To accept it.

Death of the heart –
All of them
Insisting
We'd better not.

❦ Occult power of the alphabet –
How it combines
And recombines into words
That resurrect the beloved
Every time.
                    Breaking open
The dry bones of each
Letter – seeking
The secret of life
That must be hidden inside.

❧ Grief will come to you.
   Grip and cling all you want,
   It makes no difference.

   Catastrophe? It's just waiting to happen.
   Loss? You can be certain of it.

   Flow and swirl of the world.
   Carried along as if by a dark current.

   All you can do is keep swimming;
   All you can do is keep singing.

❋ When we were young
   We feared she
   Would never come.

   Even then we felt
   His loss – felt it as lack,
   As longing.

   We never thought
   How lucky we were
   To have it all before us.

   We dreamed the beloved's
   Caress; we squirmed
   And tossed in our beds,
   Imagining pleasure.

✻ We could say No to love,
   But love itself
   Doesn't say No.

   We could say Yes
   To love,
   But it might not
   Arrive any sooner.

   Whole years going by
   In which we never
   Catch sight of the beloved,

   And then suddenly...

❧ Who needs another earth?
This one would be
Heaven enough,
Emily said,
If not for death.

But death is real, and all
That is
Flows toward its brink.

No wonder we need
Hope and courage –

What the Book brings.

❧ Reading the world
As if it were a book
Written before words —

That sparrow perched
On the withered stalk
In the garden — isn't
The bird itself
A song to the beloved

Even before it sings?

❧ Praising all creation, praising the world:
That's our job – to keep
The sweet machine of it
Running as smoothly as it can.

With words repairing, where it wears out,
Where it breaks down.

With songs and poems keeping it going.
With whispered endearments greasing its gears.

PART TWO

❧ All those years
I had only to say
Yes.
But I couldn't.

Finally, I said Maybe,
But even then
I was filled with dread.

I wanted to step carefully.
I didn't want to leap.

What if the beloved
Didn't catch me?
What if the world
Disappeared beneath my feet?

✣ That T-shirt – it smells
Of him. Don't wash it.
I need to hold it
Close.

       I want to sleep
With it near my face.

How ridiculous this is:
Grief leading me by the nose.

✤ Without a word of protest
We let death take him.
None of us spoke up –
Afraid to make a ruckus,
Afraid death might notice us.

We didn't dance or weep
Or scream our grief.
We let the beloved go
Without a song or poem,
And that diminished us.

❧ Autumn again. The leaves
   Falling. In one year, so
   Many beloveds lost,
   So many buried.
                    So many
   Gone from my sight forever;
   So many become only songs.

   Songs I can't sing yet,
   Can't even bear to hear.
   So many beloveds in one small year.

❋ That single line: a rope
   The poem tossed out
   Into the dark,
   Into the river's swirl.

   You're holding one end;
   The beloved, the other.

   Rescue is imminent.

   Too soon to say whose.

❧ When my gaze strays
From the page,
I see my mottled hand
Resting on the tabletop,
A tired thing sleeping.

When I read the poem
Aloud, my hand revives.
It wants to dance
In the air in time
To the words.
                        It wants
To make a sweeping gesture
As if clearing cobwebs
Or yanking back
A heavy curtain
To reveal the world.

❦ Human heart—
   That tender engine.

   Love revs it;
   Loss stalls it.

   What can make it
   Go again?

   The poem, the poem.

✤ To learn by heart is to learn
By hurt – grief inscribing
Its wisdom in the soft tissue.

Song you sing, poem you are –
Finger moving, precise
As a phonograph needle,
Along the groove of scar.

❧ Your Yes against all those
   Shouted noes.

   How brave you were.
   What courage it took.
   As if one self defied
   The whole cosmos.

   So what if it all took place
   Silently inside you?

❧ Space we make
With our arms –
How briefly the beloved
Rests there.

Space the poem makes
In our hearts –
Maybe forever.

❋ Words, of course, but
Also the silence
Between them.

Like the silence
Between
The beloved and you.
Silence full
Of the unspoken
As a seed is full
Of all
It will become.

No poem made only
Of silence.
No poem
Made only of words.

❋ Surrender everything. Give up
All that's precious –
That way you won't be tempted
To bicker with yourself
Over scraps you still control.

Besides, who knows the depth
Of her pity? Who knows
How far down
He can reach with his love?

❧ Loss and loss and more
Loss – that's what
The sea teaches.

The need to stay
Nimble
Against the suck
Of receding waves,
The sand
Disappearing
Under our feet.

Here, where sea
Meets shore:
The best of dancing floors.

❦ What death shatters
(Sliver in the dirt,
Shard in the heart),

Song will find
No matter
How scattered.

Poem will gather
Into its pattern.

❧ Steeling your heart,
Yet what's the use?

Already it's stolen.
Already the beloved
Has captured the castle.

How defend yourself
Against rapture?
How protect yourself
When the world
And all the words
In the Book
Conspire against you?

Better to surrender.
The beloved's beauty
Has pierced your heart,

And that's its purpose –
That's the point of it.

❧ Lingering over it,
Wanting to make it last
Longer.
                Still,
It ends.

No joy
That doesn't cease.
No life that goes on
Forever.

The poet writes
Then puts down
His pen.

The singer comes
To the end
Of her song.

Autumn now:
The leaves falling.

Beautiful world
That persists
When words stop.

Beautiful words
That lift the world
In a song of praise
That drifts
Like a leaf in a breeze.

❧ Childhood swimming hole,
   The bridge across it.
   I held on so long,
   Dangled there, afraid.
   Hoping somehow
   I could gauge
   The water's depth
   Before I let go.

   No shame in that:
   Any sane person
   Might have felt fear.

   But I was wrong: it
   Wasn't shallow or shatter.
   It was deep,
   Deeper than I could imagine.

❧ Letting go, when all you want is to hold.
Turning away, when all you want is to stay.

Almost all that's in the Book was written
On just such a day:

Someone remaining;
                    someone going away.

Someone becoming silent;
                    someone who must say.

PART THREE

❋ The hero who cuts a swath
   Through enemy ranks
   Armed with wrath –
   I'm not him.
                    Desire
   Is all I have. And grief,
   Perpetual companion
   Of love.
                    Together,
   We're a modest trio
   Serenading the beloved
   Who's shut herself up
   In the Book
   And won't come out.

   Rage and sword
   Won't open that door.
   Pick that lock with a song.

❦ Young, we waved flags
That were scarlet or black –
Pure hues that thrilled us.

We dreamed of sacrificing
Everything
In a single extravagant gesture,
Because all we had
Was ourselves
And we felt like nothing.

We had not met the beloved yet.

❦ Doesn't the soldier serve
The state? Isn't that his
Or her job? Doesn't
He dream of heroic deeds,
Or she of giving her life
To protect her family?

Who does the poet serve?
The poet serves poetry,
Whose form is the beloved,
Who asks not blood but love.

Soon the battle will begin.
Always, it's the eve of battle.
Do we have the courage we need?

The Book held close, the pages
You cherish clearly marked.
Will you be brave enough to speak?

❧ The terror and thrill
Of battle, the fear
That has you shit yourself:
Has it come to this?

Someone's beloved
Become a corpse.
A flag on a coffin
Can't raise the dead.

Or suppose he comes back
Alive, with another body
Inside him that's not.

❦ Who says there's nothing written
   On the Book's blank pages?

   Some have simply faded
   And need to be written again.

   But some are cries for love
   So shrill no ears can hear them.

   Others inscribed in invisible ink
   Because the secret's too painful.

❦ Voice of the beloved
Searching me out,
Seeking me,
                    speaking me.

Speaking herself first;
Speaking his own being
In order to awaken mine.

❁ Has the moon been up there
All these nights
And I never noticed?

A whole week with my nose
To the ground, to the grind.

And the beloved faithfully
Returning each evening
As the moon.

Where have I been?
Who has abandoned whom?

❧ Reciprocity – that's where
It starts.
           Not something
Given selflessly
Nor grabbed without regard.

The free exchange – caress
Begetting caress. Gaze
Answering gaze.
                 Across
What gulfs, voice
Responding to voice,
As poem responds to poem.

❧ Her eye and my "I":
Her gazing
Creates me.

His voice and my
Ear – I'm seized
By hearing.

How because
Of the beloved
I come into being.

Under her touch,
All of me shudders.

❧ Those pastel, candy hearts
Emblazoned with phrases:
"Be My Valentine" or
"I Luv You." How they
Simply appeared
In a little heap on your desk
Next to the inkwell
When you were in second grade.
They didn't seem to come
From any one person
But from the universe.

The wonder of it: words
Printed on the heart,
As if each heart could speak
And chose to speak of love.

❋ When I was young I wanted
So many things: gadgets
And clothes and cars.

When I was older
I wanted to travel
And eat good food.

Now I want to study
The book of the world:
Every vanishing page.

Now I want to read
The Book of the beloved
Whose every poem
Laughs at the grave.

❋ What was it the beloved
   Promised – out of
   His infinite passion,
   Out of her deepest love?

   Whatever it was,
   Eternity had no part in it.

   Sometimes only the length
   Of a single poem;

   Sometimes just a few
   Words of a song
   Disturbing the air –
   And then he's gone.

❧ Squander it all!
Hold nothing back.

The heart's a deep well.

And when it's empty,
It will fill again.

❋ Ask the tree or the house;
Ask the rose or the fire
Hydrant – everything's
Waiting for you to notice.
Everything's waiting for you
To wrap your heart around it.

That music has been playing
Since you were born.
You must be mad to resist it.
Always the beloved
Surrounds us,
Eager to dance.
All we have to do is ask.

More stores being built
On the corner. More things
To buy and sell.
                    The beloved
Is lost – she can't be
Bought; he can't be sold.

For the price of a poem
The beloved is yours again.

If you can't afford that,
Write one of your own.

❧ Lots of sorrow and a little joy.
  Lots of joy and only a bit
  Of sorrow.
                    Who can know
  The formula beforehand?

  We don't get to watch
  While it's mixed. No one tells us
  What's in it.
                    We lift it
  To our lips – azure elixir
  That burns our throats to crystal.

PART FOUR

✤ "Surprise me," the beloved said.

Command or enticement?
Flirtatious or earnest?

Tone of that voice
I no longer remember,
But I knew those words
Would rule my days.

As if the world itself spoke,
And I was supposed to answer.

❧ High Virginia summer
And where
Is the beloved?

Almost buried
By this thick green.

How can she breathe
Under such luxuriance?

Perfume of honeysuckle
And the taffy pink
Flowers of mimosa.

Humid morning –
Close as a room
With a corpse.

But the beloved's there,
Keeping still
Because of the heat.

His heart beating slow
But still beating.

❧ Sudden buildup
Of dark clouds;
Wind's roar;
Lightning
Announcing downpour.

Who says the beloved's
Appearance
Can't terrify?
Who says she can't
Arrive as a summer storm?

❧ When the beloved appears
As a daylily,
She has only one
Arc of the sun
To blossom, to blare
The orange trumpet
Of her being
Loudly into the world.

Quick, write a poem –
We must prolong her song.

❧ We poets are always
Dipping our cups
In Heraclitus's river,
Drinking its health,
Toasting it with raised
Glasses.
            We know
A single drop of it
Sanctifies an entire
Gallon of wine.

We know it's the deep
Stream of the world
And surges through
Every page of the Book.

We know the beloved
Is an otter that dives
From its banks, frolics
In its swirling currents.

Or bows above its
Shallows as a heron,
Ready to seize
The minnow of us in her beak.

✽ So many were given only
A dream of love,
So many given a glimpse,
And that from such a distance.

Who am I to be ungrateful
Who saw the beloved
Face-to-face?

❧ When the beloved
Has the blues –
No cheering her up,
No lifting him
From the dumps.

When the beloved
Is the blues,
No keeping her down,
No muffling his voice.
It sounds out
Over the radio waves –
A low moan and a high
Yell.
      She's the guitar
Sound like the train
Leaving town.
            Moan and yell –
Where is your baby bound?

❋ According to the Big Bopper
In the immortal "Chantilly
Lace," a wiggle
In the walk is one ingredient
That makes the world
Go round.

        Something
Sappho also noted
Twenty-six centuries ago
As she watched Anactoria's
Hips shift while she strolled
And wrote: "Whatever
One loves most is beautiful."

Book so full of wisdom,
Stuffed with it. Crammed
With astute observations
About anatomy in action!

❧ Beloved, with your hair
Like a cloud
That half-hides the moon.
With eyes like pools
That disprove stars and depths
In the same sentence.
With fingers delicate and precise
As brushes Angelico used
To make the Madonna smile.
With occult hands. With
Shoulders like banks of snow
The wind has sculpted.
With breasts that made Krishna
Restless all night, so nothing
Could silence his lonely flute.
With belly of wheat and sable.
With hips like the wave's swell.
With hips that are cliffs
And whose sex is the salty harbor
Of the mariner's dream,
Where he's safe at last from the sea.

for Trisha

Little fish of feeling, small
As the beloved's toes;
Little nibblers like erotic
Shivers.

Caught in the net
And hauled up on deck –
Spilled in a silver heap in your lap.

Weaves a net wide as the sky,
Yet able to catch the tiniest fish –
How does the Book do that?

❧ The poet might wish
To put a ship
In a bottle,
But what about the waves?

In the model, they're
Only blue plaster
Teased into tufts and billows.

You can't bottle
The beloved –
No matter how
Transparent and shapely
The vessel
That contains him,
How clear the glass
In which
She's encased.

Ship in a bottle
On the shelf – quite
A marvel.
            The Book
On the shelf –
Shattering what holds it,
Showering us all
With its spray.

❧ Every day brings us
Closer to parting
As all that we are
Flows
Toward the brink
Death is.

And every kiss
We give
Or get
Could be
The last one.

Opening hearts
And arms
To such an embrace:
How brave we are!

❧ Making light of the beloved –
    Laughing, not at her
    But with her,
    Laughing at death
    Even.
              Making light
    Of the beloved –
    Turning the mortal dark
    Into radiant words.

    Making light of the beloved
    Because he weighs
    Almost nothing.

    Lifting him easily
    As you lift a book;
    Balancing her
    On the tip of your tongue.

❧ Blossoms scattered in the street
As if the beloved's necklace
Broke.

      Wild night!
No time to stop
And gather each bead.

Let the Book burst asunder –
Let it be nothing but songs of love.

❋   Fate not just a pair of scissors
     Waiting at the end to cut the thread,
     But there at the beginning,
     Spinning the same thread out:
     That bright filament of song
     Whitman said connects us all –

     Spinning out that string of words
     With which we wed the world,
     With which we espouse the beloved.

     Spinning out the poem of our vow.

❧ Being being nothing
But breath

And the fog it makes
On the windowpane,

Which is a page
In the Book

On which
You write your name.

❋ To open the Book
Is to open yourself.

But to close it –
That's not so easy.

Once you know
The beloved is there
And not lost forever...

Once you've felt
All those feelings again...

Closing the Book –
It can be done.

But to close yourself?

❋ Sometimes the poem
   Changes you slowly,
   As if eroding the old life.

   You have to be patient
   With the way it unfolds –
   One line at a time.

   So unlike the beloved:
   All at once and forever.

❧ Hoarding your joys and despairs
As if they were clothes
You bought but never wore.

Look at this bright shirt:
A possibility you glimpsed
But feared to seize.

The beloved is waiting.
You have a date.
Put on that shirt before it fades.

❧ Weren't we more than
Electricity and dust?

Weren't we the hours
We lay beside
Each other?
                    Weren't we
The marks
We made on the page?

Weren't we the days
We knew we had purpose
And every step
We took was praise?

* Nazim Hikmet begins a poem
  With the phrase, "Another thing
  I didn't know I loved."
  He writes in a tone of amazement.

  He's a Turkish poet in exile.
  He's on a train in winter,
  Leaving Prague and headed
  Toward an uncertain future.
  The poem he's writing is a list
  Of things he suddenly knows
  Are precious.
                He doesn't know
  Where he's going – old man
  At the start of a long, cold ride.
  The list he recites is also long.

  As long as he keeps making that list,
  He's traveling toward the beloved.

❧ This is what was bequeathed us:
This earth the beloved left
And, leaving,
Left to us.

No other world
But this one:
Willows and the river
And the factory
With its black smokestacks.

No other shore, only this bank
On which the living gather.

No meaning but what we find here.
No purpose but what we make.

That, and the beloved's clear instructions:
Turn me into song; sing me awake.

❦ Humble dazzle
Of autumn:
These leaves
On the ground –
Each one a page
In the Book,
A poem that says:
I lived.

      I was
A small part
Of the whole
Story – this
Is my song,
This is my glory.

❧ Poem that opened you –
  The opposite of a wound.

  Didn't the world
  Come pouring through?

ABOUT THE AUTHOR

Gregory Orr was born in Albany, New York, in 1947. Among his many books are nine previous collections of poetry, including *Concerning the Book That Is the Body of the Beloved, The Caged Owl: New and Selected Poems,* and *Orpheus and Eurydice,* as well as a memoir, *The Blessing,* and a cultural study, *Poetry as Survival.* Featured on National Public Radio's *This I Believe,* he has been the recipient of fellowships from the Guggenheim Foundation and the National Endowment for the Arts, and of an Award in Literature from the American Academy of Arts and Letters.

Orr is a professor of English at the University of Virginia, where he has taught since 1975, and was the founder and first director of its Creative Writing MFA Program. He lives with his wife, the painter Trisha Orr, and his two daughters in Charlottesville, Virginia.

The Chinese character for poetry is made up of two parts: "word" and "temple." It also serves as pressmark for Copper Canyon Press.

Since 1972, Copper Canyon Press has fostered the work of emerging, established, and world-renowned poets for an expanding audience. The Press thrives with the generous patronage of readers, writers, booksellers, librarians, teachers, students, and funders—everyone who shares the belief that poetry is vital to language and living.

Major funding has been provided by:

Anonymous

Beroz Ferrell & The Point, LLC

Cynthia Hartwig and Tom Booster

Lannan Foundation

National Endowment for the Arts

Cynthia Lovelace Sears and Frank Buxton

Washington State Arts Commission

For information and catalogs:

COPPER CANYON PRESS
Post Office Box 271
Port Townsend, Washington 98368
360-385-4925
www.coppercanyonpress.org

The text is set in Dante, designed by Giovanni Mardersteig in 1954. Mardersteig was a fine printer and type designer who made his home in Verona. The titles are set in Scala Sans, designed by Martin Majoor in 1993. Book design and composition by Valerie Brewster, Scribe Typography.